3410

Winds in the Woods—
The Story of John Muir

Winds
in the Woods–
The Story of
John Muir

BY JOHN STEWART

THE WESTMINSTER PRESS/PHILADELPHIA

PUBLISHED BY THE WESTMINSTER PRESS®
PHILADELPHIA, PENNSYLVANIA

PRINTED IN THE UNITED STATES OF AMERICA

Library of Congress Cataloging in Publication Data

Stewart, John, 1920–
    Winds in the woods: the story of John Muir.

    Bibliography: p.
    Includes index.
    SUMMARY: A biography of the naturalist, geologist, inventor, adventurer, writer, and artist who gave up thoughts of engineering and medical school in favor of a life of exploring wilderness areas.
    1. Muir, John, 1838–1914—Juvenile literature.
    [1. Muir, John, 1838–1914. 2. Naturalists]
    I. Title.
QH31.M9S74   333.7′2′0924 [B] [92]   74–20708
ISBN 0–664–32556–4

To Jean and Loye Guthrie

Me ke aloha pau ole a hui hau

Preface

Storms, thunderclouds,
winds in the woods—
were welcomed as friends.
—John Muir

In his own writings John Muir refers to
the wind as though he were a part of it. On the flyleaf
of one of his sixty journals he wrote: "John Muir, Earth-
Planet, Universe." Like the wind, he was at home with
nature—an important part of Earth-Planet, Universe.
His own words, from journals and letters, set this mood
for each chapter of the life story.

John Muir, known as the "Father of our National
Parks," found fascination in all of nature, from bees to
bears and meadows to mountains. Often he wished he
were an atom within the glaciers he studied so that he
might explain their innermost secrets. To him the wind
was a unifying and diversifying symbol, and he liked
nothing more than to take his blanket and a few slices

of dry bread into the wilderness. His guide was the tone and language of the wind.

From the windswept coast of Scotland, his birthplace, across the windswept seas to America, came John Muir. He was a man who lived close to God through his understanding of nature.

He was a self-taught naturalist, a geologist, an inventor, adventurer, writer, and artist. No other writer can truly capture this man's love of beauty, his dedication to preserving nature, his zeal for adventure. If I can but stir winds in the woods for the reader, perhaps our priceless heritage—nature—will not be destroyed.

J.S.

Covina, California

1

Some of my grandfathers
must have been born on a muirland,
for there is heather in me . . .

As a boy John Muir roamed
the moors of Scotland

1

John Muir felt that man's inventions blinded him, so at the age of twenty-nine he turned to God's inventions—nature. He always believed that there must be a close man-nature relationship and he set out to discover it. Man's lack of regard for nature, he felt, would in time destroy man himself.

Muir turned to the wilderness. He spent forty-four adventurous years with winds in the woods, seeking a solution to the mysteries of life.

He wrote to his brother in 1873: "Most people who are born into the world remain babies all their lives, their development being arrested like sun-dried seeds." He referred to their father, who had never approved of John's closeness to nature.

John was born to the wilderness. His native home, Dunbar, Scotland, faced the rugged North Sea. It was a seaport town with moss-covered ruins, meadows, and seemingly endless wooded country surrounding it. Dunbar was steeped in over a thousand years of folklore, superstitions, and legends.

It was into this windswept environment that John Muir was born on April 21, 1838. By the time Daniel and Ann Muir's auburn-haired, blue-eyed boy was three years old, his schooling had begun. He had learned to read and spell with the help of his Grandfather Gilrye and shop signs along Dunbar's crooked, cobbled streets.

Reddish-gray stone houses with glistening purple slate roofs contrasted sharply with the ruins of old Dunbar Castle. But the sea wind didn't seem to care as it blew blossom fragrances in spring, dust and sand in summer, multicolored leaves in autumn, and refuse from the sea in winter.

John's life can be divided into four periods: The spring of his life he considered a period of seedtime, bearing the firstfruits of his choice of nature over civilization. The summer of his life cleared away any doubts about his future and began more than twenty years of exploration, observation, analysis, and discovery. Adventure and excitement carried over into his autumn years. The fourth period of his life, like winter, was harsh and drove him toward stormy action in the field of conservation.

Stormy action was the key to John Muir's whole life. "The very devil's in that boy," his father often said. John's first teacher, Mungo Siddons, no doubt agreed with that description. The high-walled Davel Brae schoolyard often became a battleground for opposing armies. Blue bonnets stuffed with sand, stones, or snow were used for ammunition. After each battle, friend and foe returned to class. Sometimes the warfare continued in the classroom. Mr. Siddons then used his switch, but usually softened the punishment with currants and gooseberries.

After school, footraces up the brae were a favorite sport. John, who usually won, lost one day and was shamed before his friends.

"Johnny got beat by a girl," the boys teased. But John was not one to take such a defeat easily. Every moment that he could slip away from home he spent holding his breath and running up the brae. Before long he was the winner of every footrace.

Running in those days was not always for racing. It was sometimes for fear of being caught by a "dandy doctor" and sold to the medical school in Edinburgh. The crimes of Burke and Hare had spread throughout Scotland. John had no intention of letting a "dandy doctor" clap a sticky-plaster over his mouth so he could not call out for help, then hide him under a long black cloak. Nobody was going to sell him to Dr. Hare. If doctors wanted to learn how people were made, they weren't going to cut up Johnny Muir to find out.

Doctors were feared by children in those days. After all, who could tell a "dandy doctor" from a real doctor? They both wore long black cloaks.

When John was born he already had two sisters: Margaret, who was four years old, and Sarah, age two. Then when John was two years old his brother, David, was born. John, being the first son, felt a need to protect his brother and sisters from harm. Especially from doctors. When David was a few days old, the doctor vaccinated him. John watched while the doctor scratched David's arm until it bled. John could not understand how his mother could just hold the baby and let the doctor do such a thing. The little boy ran to the doctor and jumped high enough to bite his arm.

John was five when his brother, Daniel, Jr., was born. And by the time John was ready for grammar school, 1846, his twin sisters, Annie and Mary, had arrived.

Grammar school left little time for him to admire the twins. Schoolmaster Lyon made the children learn three lessons a day in English, Latin, and French as well as lessons in history, geography, arithmetic, and spelling.

13

Those who didn't learn were soundly thrashed, for teachers then believed that a smarting of the skin smarted the brain.

That was not all John Muir had to learn. After breakfast of oatmeal porridge; lunch of broth, mutton, and weak tea; and supper of boiled potatoes and barley scones, his father drilled him in Bible verses and hymns. By the time John was eleven, he knew the New Testament and most of the Old by heart. Daniel Muir loved his children, but he was very stern. Ann Muir was understanding and wise, and like all mothers, healed all wounds both physical and spiritual.

But not every hour was study and discipline. Although their father did not want his boys to leave the yard after school, John and David ran off every chance they had. A good adventure was worth the good thrashing they would receive if their father found out.

Dunbar Castle was their favorite playground. John loved to climb the crumbling crags and peaks or go searching the ruins for witches, ghosts, and boowuzzies.

There was a calmer side to John Muir too: his love of nature, daisied fields, nest-hunting, and the songs of skylarks and mavises. He loved the rugged seashore, where he explored tide pools for shells, crabs, seaweed— whatever surprise the sea had washed up. But most of all he loved the woods and the birds.

"In our back yard," John recalled years later, "there were three Elm trees and in the one nearest the house a pair of robin-redbreasts had their nest. When the young were almost able to fly, a troop of the celebrated 'Scottish Grays' visited Dunbar, and three or four of the fine horses were lodged in our stable. When the soldiers were polishing their swords and helmets, they happened

14

to notice the nest, and just as they were leaving, one of them climbed the tree and robbed it. With sore sympathy we watched the young birds as the hard-hearted robber pushed them one by one beneath his jacket—all but two that jumped out of the nest and tried to fly, but they were easily caught as they fluttered on the ground, and were hidden away with the rest. The distress of the bereaved parents, as they hovered and screamed over the frightened crying children they so long had loved and sheltered and fed, was pitiful to see; but the shining soldier rode grandly away on his big gray horse, caring only for the few pennies the young songbirds would bring and the beer they would buy, while we all, sisters and brothers, were crying and sobbing. I remember, as if it happened this day, how my heart fairly ached and choked me."

Soon John, David, and Sarah were to be taken from their Scotland nest. One evening, as the boys were studying their lessons across the street at Grandfather Gilrye's, their father brought the news.

"Put away your lessons. In the morning we're going to America!"

John was excited. He had read about the great wilderness across the ocean. "David," he cried, "all those woods, mountains, gold, and—"

"And don't forget the birds' nests and lakes and—" David stopped for a moment, then in a quieter voice added, "Indians!"

"Well, they're better than the old dandy doctors," John said.

Both boys stopped talking and looked at their grandfather. There was loneliness in his tired old eyes.

"Ah, poor laddies," he said, his voice trembling,

15

"you'll find something else over the sea besides gold and birds' nests and freedom from lessons. You'll find plenty of hard work." He shook his head sadly, then gave John and David each a gold coin for a keepsake.

And so it was that on the morning of February 19, 1849, Daniel Muir, two of his sons, and one daughter sailed from Glasgow, Scotland, for New York City. Ann Muir and the other children, Margaret, Daniel, Jr., and the twins, would sail after a home had been established for them in America.

2

Everything new and pure
in the very prime of the spring
when Nature's pulses were beating
highest and mysteriously
keeping time with our own!
Young hearts, young leaves,
flowers, animals,
the winds and the streams
and the sparkling lake, all wildly,
gladly rejoicing together!

2

It took Daniel Muir and his three children six weeks and three days to reach New York Harbor. Much of the crossing Daniel spent below nursing seasickness. All of Sarah's voyage was spent in her bunk. But not so John and David. They were on deck watching the sailors, learning the names of ropes and sails, and a few lusty sailor songs. They played with Irish, German, French, and Scandinavian boys.

Stiff gales whipped the great sails and caused food boxes to slide about the decks. Such excitement the boys had never known. "We were flying to our fortunes on the wings of the winds, carefree as thistle seeds," John later wrote.

Wings of the winds slowed down once the Muirs reached New York. It had been Daniel's idea to settle in Upper Canada's backwoods. But in Buffalo, New York, he talked to farmers who told him that land in Wisconsin was easier to cultivate.

Daniel Muir homesteaded in Kingston, Wisconsin. Their 160 acres, a quarter section of land, delighted John. It was surrounded by woods and meadows, and a small lake glistened in the bright sunlight. Fountain Lake it was called then, but it is now known as Muir Lake.

John's formal schooling had stopped and the lessons of nature took over. The small shanty in which they were

19

to live was built in a day with the help of friendly neighbors.

John's first sight of the farm was thrilling, not because of the land or the shanty—he and David had spotted a blue jay's nest. "Come on," he shouted to David, and shinned up the tree.

"Move over." David was right beside his brother on the limb.

"Our first discovery in America," John whispered, his eyes shining as they looked at the green eggs.

Mother and Father Blue Jay did not take kindly to the boys and became screaming flights of anger. "We didn't come to rob you," John called out, and climbed down from the tree.

The boys raced into the woods looking for more birds. Four clear, high whistles followed by a trill on the same pitch greeted them.

"A field sparrow." John glanced around, hoping to see it.

"Listen." David stopped. "Hear them?"

"Fearnot—cheerup—fearnot—cheerup—cheerup," came several loud bird voices.

"Robins." John ran ahead of his brother into the thick of the woods.

"No, over here," David called. "A redwing blackbird."

The woods and meadows were alive with birds, the air sweet with their singing. The boys searched trees, grass, meadow, and lakeshore, plunging heart first into the lush wilderness.

The wilderness of Wisconsin was to John a place of wonder and beauty. Here the lessons of nature were lessons of love and not book lessons to be beaten into

20

him. Work had to be done, but until November when their mother and the rest of the family would come, John and David would have a lot of time to explore.

Sarah's job was to cook and keep the shanty clean. Daniel and a hired hand tilled the soil with the help of oxen, and of course John and David.

John's joy was doubled when his father bought Jack, an Indian pony, for the boys.

"Take him to the meadow and learn to ride," their father said.

John mounted the pony. He held tight to the mane, and Jack galloped off. Without bridle and saddle, John bounced up and down, mostly up. "Whoa—whoa, Jack!" John cried out. Jack stopped but John kept going, right over the pony's head.

"Your turn, David." John watched his younger brother bounce up and down. When David yelled, "Whoa, Jack!" he too flew over the pony's head.

Before long both boys learned to ride at breakneck speed. They learned to guide Jack by leaning from side to side and putting light pressure to his flanks with their knees.

The boys taught themselves to swim in Fountain Lake. All this and heavy farm work toughened their muscles. This developed the strength and endurance that John would need as a man of the mountains.

John, David, and their father set to work that first summer building the new house. The finest lumber was brought from Milwaukee for their two-and-a-half-story, eight-room house. By October they moved into it. Sarah worked very hard getting everything ready for the arrival of Mother and the younger children.

A month later, Ann, Danny, Margaret, and the twins

21

arrived. Once again the Muirs were nested together. But now that the family was together, life became extremely hard for the boys. John recalled Grandfather Gilrye's words, *You'll find plenty of hard work.* They worked from four in the morning until after dark in the evening.

Daniel continued his fatherly habit of thrashing the boys for what he considered to be misdeeds. Even when John had done nothing wrong, he felt the switch. Once John protested his innocence and was backed up by David.

"Well"—Daniel dropped the switch—"maybe you did nothing wrong, but I don't doubt you deserved it anyway."

Work and whippings made John want to escape from the house to the freedom of nature. He no longer went to school, but he borrowed books from neighbors to keep up his education. This did not please Daniel, for he believed that all the lessons a boy needed could be learned from the Bible.

After Bible lessons, John sat up reading until his father would say, "John, go to bed." As time went by, John continued to stay up and read, and his father grew tired of telling him to go to bed.

"John, why must I always order you to bed?"

"Father, I like to read, I want to learn and—"

"Very well. If you *must* read, get up as early in the morning as you want to, but now—*go to bed!*"

John knew that his father must always be obeyed. From then on, right after Bible lessons he went to bed without being told. But much to his father's surprise, John rose each morning at one.

3

Making some bird or beast
go lame the rest of its life
is a sore thing on one's conscience,
at least nothing to boast of,
and it has no religion in it.

THE WILD PIGEON.

From a child's book of birds
printed in 1852—when
John Muir was fourteen

3

All Wisconsin nature thrilled John, but the biggest thrill was his excitement at seeing flocks of passenger pigeons.

"Look, David!" John shouted and pointed across the lake toward a dark cloud moving swiftly in the direction of the farm.

"Nothin' to be scared of," said Lawson, a neighbor boy who was sharing John's first Fourth of July. "They're just passenger pigeons."

"What bonnie birds." David pointed to the red streaked with gold that seemed to fill the sky.

"And green around the neck." John had never seen anything so beautiful.

"Those are the males," Lawson said with authority. "They eat grain, and at night so many of 'em roost on a single branch of a tree that they break it clean off."

"Must be millions of them," David guessed as the flock flew down, then up, seeming to follow the leader in a game with the flow of the wind.

"Make mighty good pigeon pie," Lawson said as he broke off a low branch and began knocking the birds out of trees and swatting them out of the air.

"What are you doing?" John took the stick away from Lawson.

"Killin' 'em." Lawson grabbed back the stick.

"Why?" John and David asked in unison.

"'Cause they destroy grain. People kill 'em and sell 'em. Whole barrels are shipped to Chicago and New York. Bet my father'll let the pigs out to eat their fill. Everybody does. Saves havin' to slop the hogs when passenger pigeons are around."

John didn't say anything more—he felt sick. It wasn't right to destroy such beautiful creatures. Someday there wouldn't be a single passenger pigeon left.

John's thoughts were right. Ironically, John Muir died the same year that the last passenger pigeon died. Of all the birds John knew, these were his favorite.

John's favorite pastime of being with nature was short-lived. By the time he was twelve he was put behind a plow. He cut trees from the fields and had to chop out the stumps. Sixteen hours a day, summer and winter, were spent working.

By 1857, hard work had made Fountain Lake Farm the most beautiful and productive farm in the area. But Daniel Muir was not a man to remain content. He bought 320 acres, a half section, of uncultivated land and started all over on the Muirs' second farm at Hickory Hill.

John had reached the age of twenty and, as the eldest son, was given the hardest jobs.

"We'll need a well," Daniel said one evening after Bible-reading. "You'll start digging in the morning, John."

The first ten feet of the digging went easily, then John came to sandstone. "I can't dig any farther," he said.

His father closed his eyes, bowed his head and quoted the Bible: " 'I give waters in the wilderness, and rivers in the desert, to give drink to my people, my chosen.' The Lord will show you the way."

26

"But how?" John looked into the hole he had dug and shook his head.

"A chisel, a hammer, muscles, and the will of the Lord," came the sharp reply.

From sunup to sundown John chipped away, week after week. The hole was only three feet around and John had to work in a cramped position. Chips were hauled up in a bucket, as was John at noon. Then after lunch he was lowered down and not brought up until time for dinner.

"I'm down almost eighty feet," he announced one evening, "but there just isn't any water."

Daniel Muir glanced gravely at his son and shook his head. "And the Lord said, 'If ye have faith as a grain of mustard seed . . .' "

"I have faith, Father, but faith is not doing the digging!"

The following day his father lowered John into the well. The farther down John went, the tighter his chest felt. His throat burned and he began coughing.

John fell out of the bucket. His head spun and his legs were like water. "Help me," he cried out. "I—I can't breathe!"

"Get in the bucket," his father's voice commanded.

John leaned toward the bucket and fell over the edge head first. The last thing he remembered was a strange tingling in his whole body. Then blackness engulfed him.

When John opened his eyes he saw clear blue sky and breathed deeply of clean air. The sharpness of fresh air stabbed painfully at his lungs.

"We'd best get you into bed," Daniel said. "I'll have to learn what the trouble is down there. Don't worry,

John, you can go back down tomorrow."

A neighbor farmer, William Duncan, came by to see the Muirs and learned of John's trouble.

"What could be wrong?" Daniel asked.

"Only by the grace of God is Johnny alive," Farmer Duncan said slowly. "It's chokedamp. Happens in mines when carbonic acid settles on the bottom."

"What can we do?" Daniel glanced at John. "We need water."

"Well"—Farmer Duncan smiled at John—"after a couple days' bed rest you can go down again, but . . ."

"A couple of days!" Daniel shouted.

"My friend"—Farmer Duncan turned to Daniel—"chokedamp is a killer—let the boy's lungs have a rest. Then in a couple of days he can go down again, but throw water down the shaft first. That'll take up the gas. Might tie a bundle of hay on a rope and dangle it up and down to take down some fresh air."

Two days later John returned to the well and continued to chip away until he worked down another ten feet, and then with a stroke of his hammer against the chisel he was rewarded with a rush of cold, clear water.

4

I used to envy the father
of our race, dwelling as he did
in contact with the new-made fields
and plants of Eden; but
I do so no more, because I have
discovered that I also live
in "creation's dawn."

One of young John's inventions—
the student desk clock
that turned book pages
automatically—was handcarved
of wood during midnight hours

4

John Muir worked hard, but he made time for reading. During his lunchtime, he studied. He would get up in the mornings as early as one o'clock. He taught himself simple mathematics, algebra, geometry, and trigonometry. He read Cowper, Milton, and Shakespeare.

Yet, all was not study and reading—John loved to invent. He built a workshop in the basement, directly under his father's bedroom. His first task was to make a self-setting sawmill.

"And just what do you think you're doing?" Daniel Muir asked, awakened by the noise.

"You said I could get up as early as I liked."

"True—true—I did say so, but I did not expect you to get up at one o'clock in the morning!"

"A promise, Father, is a—"

"I know—and I'll not go back on my word so long as you do your regular share of the chores."

John had won. Even so, it was not easy for him. In winter he pushed back his frost-stiffened blanket and tiptoed down the stairs. His breathing created tiny clouds in the cold. In summer, the heat was unbearable. He was sure of only one thing—not to breathe was the most unbearable of all.

John created a clock with bits of wood carved from hickory. When he finally had his clock put together, it

31

not only pointed to the time and struck the hour but it told the day and month. This clock also, by means of cogwheels and levers, tipped a bed on end at a set time. John was afraid to let his father see it. He hid his great invention in the attic.

Daniel Muir, always a religious man, had become almost a fanatic. He no longer played his violin in the evenings. But when he was away from home preaching, the family relaxed. His daughters brought out embroidery to work on. Laughter filled the room when John hummed like a bagpipe and danced a Scottish jig. Then their father would storm into the house, blotting out all their pleasures.

"It's a sin to be carryin' on so," he bellowed one evening. "And as for you, John Muir, come with me!" He marched his son up to the attic. "What," he demanded, pointing to the clock, "is that contraption?"

John explained his invention and gave his father a demonstration.

"A lot of wasted time. If you worked as hard at religion as you work on nonsense, you'd be better off." But despite his objection, Daniel had John set the clock up in the parlor.

John had grown into a strong young man, and he grew a reddish-brown beard that matched his unruly hair. His interest in nature too had grown stronger. His mind and hands, always busy, created another clock. This one he shaped like a scythe, and he carved smaller scythes and arrows for the parts. A sheaf of arrows formed the pendulum. Carefully he carved "All Flesh Is Grass" above the face of the clock. Whether the Bible verse or the overall inventiveness and imagination pleased Daniel,

John never learned, but this clock became his father's pride.

When John was twenty-one, he made a huge clock with four dials. The main hand on each dial measured fourteen feet in length.

Daniel refused to allow John to put it under a gable of their barn. "You'll have the farm overrun with strangers," he objected.

"Then I'll put it up in the black oak—"

"You'll put it nowhere! It's a sin, that's what it is. Why, every time I go into Portage, people ask what you're comin' up with next."

"But—"

"People are saying you're weird and invent freaks engineered by the devil," Daniel shouted. "Now get to the plowing!"

John hid his disappointment, but thought to himself that if Father did more plowing and less preaching, they would all be happier.

John came up with several inventions, including a barometer, several thermometers, hygrometers, pyrometers, and a field thermometer so sensitive it could pick up a temperature change if an animal or a human passed within four feet of it.

John's mind was as sensitive as his field thermometer. One summer evening when he was twenty-two he went for a long walk. He had to be alone to think and to come to a decision, now that he was a man. He strolled to his favorite oak tree by the road and sat down. He picked up a piece of wood and began whittling. He would have left Hickory Hill Farm long before if it weren't for his mother, sisters, and brothers. Now he could not accept his father's injustices. He needed family affection, but he also needed freedom.

"Hello there, Johnny," Farmer Duncan called from his cart.

John had been so deep in thought that he had not heard the rumble of the cart wheels. "Hello." John stopped whittling.

"New invention?" Farmer Duncan asked as he jumped from the cart and sat beside John.

"No."

"Sure beats me how you can take a piece of wood and create such wonders. That's why I came up here, Johnny."

"Something I can do for you?" John asked.

"Well, no—that is, not exactly for me. But there is something I want you to do for yourself—"

"I don't—"

"Johnny Muir, stop interrupting and let me speak my piece. You've whittled some mighty fine inventions."

John felt embarrassed. "They're just things made of wood."

"That's the whole point. Why, they're original creations, Johnny. Now I want—"

"Sure, but where'll that get me. My father—"

"Will you let me say what I've got to say?" Farmer Duncan paused and glanced at John. "Those inventions of yours will get you to Madison for the State Fair come September."

John looked at his friend and grinned.

"Johnny, when you exhibit your inventions, you'll get more offers from machine shops than you can handle." Farmer Duncan climbed back into his cart.

"I'll think about it," John said.

34

"Think hard, Johnny. You just tell your folks and go."
Farmer Duncan flipped the reins and clucked his horses
into action.

John thought about it, tossing and turning all that
night. By morning he had made his decision.

When breakfast was over, Daniel started issuing work
orders for the day.

"I'm not going into the field, Father. I'm going to
Madison." John felt a mixture of strength and pride, yet
his cheeks warmed with color.

"Madison." Daniel placed his hands on the table and
pushed himself to his feet.

"To the State Fair." John looked up at his father. "I'll
exhibit my inventions, and when the Fair's over I'll go
to work in a machine shop."

It was as though John had issued a proclamation of
freedom for everyone. They all began talking at once.

Daniel Muir's fist came down hard on the table.
"Enough of this clackin'. John is stayin' here to work the
farm. I must devote all my time to the church—he
knows that."

Silence crashed through the room for a few seconds.

"I'm leaving this morning, Father."

"You're a man now. Do as you please." Daniel went
into his study.

John's sister Maggie jumped out of her chair. "I'll
help you pack."

"Let me drive you to the station." David clapped a
hand on John's shoulder.

His brothers and sisters all found something to do to
help. John saw that his mother was still sitting quietly
at the table. He crossed the room and put his arms
around her. "I'm sorry, Mother, but I—"

"I'm proud of you," she said, and patted his hand. "But you'll need some money."

"I have ten dollars from my own crop and Grandfather Gilrye's gold piece. I'll be fine."

"Go to your father, John. I know he's been hard on you all these years, but he's a good man. In his strange way he loves you." She nodded toward the study door and smiled.

John tapped lightly on the study door. When no reply came, he opened it. Daniel, seated at his desk, the Bible open before him, did not look up.

"Will you wish me luck, Father?"

Daniel kept his head bowed toward the Bible. His voice, heavy with anger, finally came. "I'll not wish you luck. If you do this sinful thing, you do it against my wishes." He closed the Bible and stood facing his son. Above two bristling beards, two pairs of blue eyes stared silent determination at each other.

"Very well, Father," John almost whispered. "I should like to know that if I ever need help, I can write to—"

"Depend on no one." Daniel's lips barely parted. He shook his head and slowly turned to the window. "Depend only on yourself."

John had learned stubbornness from his father, gentleness from his mother. He was glad his father had turned away. John would have been embarrassed if Daniel had seen the tears clouding his vision.

5

Toiling in the treadmills of life
we hide from the lessons of Nature. . . .
Civilized man chokes his soul as
the heathen Chinese their feet.

A muleback party in the Grand Canyon
escapes "the treadmills of life"
just as Muir did in the wilds that
he explored and fought to preserve

5

John was warmly greeted at the Fair. He set up his inventions in a booth and, as Farmer Duncan had predicted, he was a success.

The crowd's greatest interest was in what John called his early-rising machine. He had two young boys pretend to be asleep in the bed. John set the mechanism and waited.

Wheels creaked, levers groaned, and suddenly the bed tipped upward and the two boys were dumped to their feet.

Viewers laughed, cheered, and applauded, not only John's genius but his warm humor and enthusiasm. Newspaper reporters wrote glowing reports about a Wisconsin farm boy who attracted all the attention at Fine Arts Hall.

John won a fifteen-dollar prize and a diploma. But John's greatest prize was the friendship of Professor Ezra Slocum Carr and his wife, Jeanne. Their son Allie was one of the boys who had helped John in his demonstrations.

"There's my mother." Allie pointed to a young woman in a lavender-and-gray hoopskirt.

"She's a very charming lady," John said.

"Come on and meet her—she's a lot of fun." Allie ran to the edge of the platform.

"Seems you've impressed all of Madison"—Mrs. Carr

smiled up at John—"especially the youngsters."

John felt his face redden. "Thank you, Mrs. Carr."

"Do you plan to attend the university, Mr. Muir?"

"Sure would like to."

"Why don't you speak to Dean Stirling. I'm sure something could be arranged." Mrs. Carr turned to her son. "Come right home when Mr. Muir is through with his demonstrations."

College cost money and John simply didn't have it. But, he thought, how wonderful it would be to be able to attend college.

College had to wait. A man named Wiard offered John a job in his machine shop at Prairie du Chien, Wisconsin. John went with Mr. Wiard only to discover the machine shop too small to really teach him anything. He then worked for room and board with a kindly family named Pelton.

Within a few months John returned to Madison and went to see Dean Stirling.

"Just what schooling have you had, Mr. Muir?" The dean leaned back in his chair and stared at John.

"Very little, sir." John's stomach seemed to crawl with fear. His heart trembled while his brain kept reminding him how ignorant he must appear. Yet, when his mouth finished telling of the ways he had kept up with his studies, John's eyes saw a smile on the dean's face.

After what seemed an eternity of silence, Dean Stirling leaned forward. "Welcome to the University of Wisconsin," he said simply.

During John's two and a half years at the university, he worked in the fields during summer vacations. He managed to earn enough money for books and supplies,

40

and to pay thirty-two dollars a year to the college. As for food, John lived on fifty cents a week.

One winter John taught in an old log school during the day and studied at night. His subjects did not follow a regular college course. John studied subjects he felt would be of use to him—chemistry, physics, mathematics, Latin, and Greek. His favorite studies were in geology and botany.

By the spring of 1863 the restlessness, so much a part of John's character, took possession of him. The Civil War had a depressing effect on him. So many of his school friends either had been drafted into the army or had enlisted.

In a letter to his sister Sarah he wrote: "This war seems farther from a close than ever. How strange that a country with so many schools and churches should be so desolated by so unsightly a monster. Leaves have their time to fall! and though indeed there is a kind of melancholy present when they, withered and dead, are plucked from their places and made the sport of the gloomy autumn wind, yet we hardly deplore their fate, because there is nothing unnatural in it. . . . But may the same be said of the slaughtered upon a field?"

John's mental battlefield was soldiered with indecision. He truly loved inventing things, he enjoyed the thought of becoming a doctor, and he worshiped nature. For a time he settled on the University of Michigan to study medicine. Yet the draft, despite victories at Gettysburg and Vicksburg, could still claim him. Should he run to Canada to avoid the draft? So many young men did. But John could not bring himself to run away.

"John," his mother said on one of his visits home, "why don't you choose a profession and stick with it?"

"I've thought of becoming a doctor, but . . ."

"Maybe a minister? You know your father would like that."

"No, Mother. I'm hungry deep down here." John touched his chest. "My soul hungers. I am on the world —but am I in it?"

The rest of his family was of little help. Sarah reminded him that they expected great things of him. Sarah's husband, David Galloway, said, "John, serve mankind. Invent machines to lighten man's burdens."

John's brother David urged, "Forget weeds and trees. What you need, John, is a wife. Settle down and go into a business of some kind. Take your place in civilization."

"What," John answered, "has civilization to brag about? It drives its victims in flocks, represses the growth of individuality. I want something more than the treadmill of toiling to eat and eating to toil."

When the first anemone struggled through the earth, its silken head announcing the spring of 1864, John announced that he was leaving home.

"Where will you go?" his mother asked.

"I don't know. The whole world is out there—I'll find a place to rest."

John's draft number had not been called and he felt free to wander. He rambled through Michigan to Lake Superior and across into Canada. He felt like a young bee on its first excursion to a flower garden.

He moved his long legs in an easy rhythm and breathed deeply of nature's clear, clean air. His food was bread—dried to prevent mold—or oatmeal flakes scorched on hot campfire stones, and tea.

All was not freedom during the years in Canada from

1864 to 1866. He worked in a broom factory in Meaford, Canada. Just as he was beginning to think he was buried in work he was never to escape, the factory burned down.

In April of 1866, John Muir arrived in Indianapolis, Indiana. He went to work for a carriage-parts manufacturer.

The other men soon became friends with John, and his inventions to make life easier for them brought him advances in pay and position.

"You're a top man," Judson Osgood, the manager, said one day. "You're about due to be made my head foreman. And—who knows—before long you could become a partner."

The clang, whir, and roar of machinery was like music, but to John not nearly so sweet as the music of birds and brooks. One he knew was the tune of the money-maker, but the other was the symphony of nature.

"Someday," he told Riley, a close friend at work, "I'm going to take a long, long trip into the real wilderness."

"That's just great, John, but how about a short trip to this machine?" Riley laughed. "This new belt needs readjusting."

"Sure." John used a slender metal file to unlace the joining. "Spring's just around the corner, you can hear—"

Suddenly John stopped talking, the sharp file slipped and flew into his face, piercing the edge of his right eye. He cupped his hand over his eye and walked to the window.

"What's wrong?" Riley rushed to his side.

John took his hand away, and milky white, aqueous humor dripped down onto his hand. Slowly the setting sunlight on the meadow faded from his right eye's sight. Then the scene through his left eye faded also as a result of shock.

"John"—Riley put his hand on John's shoulder—"what is it?"

"I'm blind!"

6

How little note is taken
of the deeds of Nature! . . .
Who publishes the sheet-music
of winds or the written music
of water written in river-lines? . . .
And what record is kept
of Nature's colors—the clothes
she wears—of her birds,
her beasts—her livestock?

6

"Sunshine and winds play in the gardens of God and I will never see them," John said to his doctor.

"Nonsense, Mr. Muir. We can replace the aqueous humor. Your right eye will see again." The doctor tried to assure him.

"And the left eye?" John asked, not all assured.

"Sympathy and shock is all. A few days and the sight will come back."

For four long, fright-filled weeks John lay in a darkened room—waiting. Each day the window shades were raised an inch. Each day brought friends and flowers. Gradually John saw them as hazy blurs, then as blurred shapes, and finally as clear images. His sight had returned.

"How about coming back to the shop?" Judson Osgood asked John. "The new plant is about ready. That foreman job and a good raise are yours."

John smiled at his employer. "Mr. Osgood, this morning I walked in the woods. I saw the beauty of God's creations. How softly the gray clouds filtered the sunlight, how sweet the sights and sounds of nature."

"Yes. April is nice. Look, Mr. Muir, I don't expect you to come back to work tomorrow—another couple of weeks and—"

John shook his head. "No, Mr. Osgood, a couple of

weeks or a couple of months—it wouldn't matter."

"I don't understand."

"It's as though I've risen from the grave, Mr. Osgood. This morning I realized God has to nearly kill us to teach us lessons."

"Think about it, please," Judson Osgood insisted.

"I have. I could become a millionaire, but I think I'd rather be a tramp! Thank you for your offer." John extended his hand. "I won't be back to the shop."

Judson shook John's hand. "You could be a great man. We're going to miss you. Where will you go?"

"My new address, Mr. Osgood, will be the Universe."

John went home to Hickory Hill Farm to tell his parents his plans. Daniel said very little, and what he did say was not encouraging. "Wandering around like some devil-possessed heathen will bring you to a no-good end."

His mother's smile, a little sad, was warm. "It's always been your nature to be restless," she sighed slightly. "But I understand. Sarah and Margaret are married now. Joanna plans to be a teacher like the twins. You need not worry about us. Just be careful, Johnny."

"I'll miss all of you." John sat beside his mother. "I'll walk through many cold shadows of loneliness. But there's so much for me to see and to learn in the University of the Wilderness."

"Where will you go?"

John took a map from his pocket and spread it out on the floor. "Well, I'll take a train to Louisville, Kentucky. From there I'll walk right through Kentucky, Tennessee, the Carolinas"—he traced with his finger on the map— "and Georgia. From Georgia I'll take a coastal steamer to Florida."

48

"That's a long way, Johnny." Tears glistened in his mother's eyes.

"Oh, I plan to go farther. I want to go to South America."

"Johnny, I'm worried—what if you are robbed?"

John folded the map. "I won't carry much money. I gave David money to mail to me in Savannah, Georgia. I figure I won't need it until I take the steamer for Florida."

That night John wrote on the flyleaf of an empty journal:

"John Muir, Earth-Planet, Universe."

John arrived in Louisville early one morning in September, 1867. He walked straight through the city. A strange sight he was with his rubber pack of only the barest necessities slung over one shoulder and his plant press slung over the other.

Kentucky's great oaks spread their arms in welcome. Winds whispered friendly greetings through the pines. Even the flowers seemed to rejoice at this tall man with the wavy, red-brown hair and beard. He was at home with nature. For the first time in his twenty-nine years of life, John truly felt free.

After six days of wandering freely through the wildest, leafiest world he had ever seen, John reached the caves of Kentucky. He listened to the music of strong, cold wind coming from deep in the cave's gargantuan throat.

"What you doin', stranger?"

John glanced up at a lanky man standing over him. A long weed dangled from the man's mouth. "Listening to the wind," John answered.

"Some mighty good huntin' hereabouts." The man scratched his head. "Where's your gun?"

"I'm not a hunter. I'm interested in gathering specimens of flowers and—"

"Only fools mess around with weeds." The man shook his head in disgust.

John only smiled, content to be one of God's fools. He thought how like his father in attitude this man was. "So long." He waved to the stranger and walked on.

By September 11, John began his climb into the Cumberland Mountains of Tennessee. "My first real mountains," he said out loud.

His joy was overshadowed by the sight of many deserted farms, and people who were desperately poor. Worst of all to John were the neglected orchards. Roving bands of guerrillas roamed the area, plundering their fellowmen like wild beasts. Many of the mountaineers distilled moonshine. Strangers were feared and hated as government revenue men or Yankee peddlers.

John pushed through the beautiful Georgia cypress woods and on to Savannah. He marveled at the live oaks gracefully draped with Spanish moss easily eight feet long. He passed the Bonaventure Cemetery on his way in to town. David would have sent the money by now.

"Sorry," the postal clerk said. "Maybe tomorrow."

John strolled down to the beach and gathered a few specimens of the yellow solidagos that covered the low dunes. Then he wandered about trying to find a safe place for the night. He drifted by homeless men and heard their rough voices. They would kill a man for a copper penny, he thought.

The Bonaventure Cemetery, a perfect place. He crossed a muddy stream just outside the cemetery. Under the shelter of sparkleberry bushes, he settled down for the night.

50

Every day for a week John went to the post office. Every day he got the same answer, "Maybe tomorrow." Every night he slept safely among the tombstones.

Finally David's letter and the money arrived. John sent a box of specimens and a letter of thanks to David. Then he ate a hearty meal and boarded a packet boat for Florida's Gulf Coast.

John stopped at a Cedar Keys sawmill. "Any lumber schooners leaving for Havana, Cuba?" he asked the mill-owner, Mr. Hodgson.

"In a couple weeks. You could work here until then if you'd like."

John was happy to earn some money, but one day, about a week later, he stopped pushing a log through the blade. His head throbbed, and every muscle and nerve in his body felt numb. One moment he was freezing, the next his body seemed to be on fire. Then came darkness.

When John opened his eyes, he saw the kind face of Mrs. Hodgson. "Well, feeling better now, are we?" she asked, and smiled.

"What happened?" John's voice was weak.

"You had a touch of malaria." She smoothed the covers around him.

"Havana . . . the boat . . . how long . . ."

"I'm afraid you just missed one, but there'll be another soon. What you need now is plenty of rest." Mrs. Hodgson went out of the room.

John soon felt strong enough to walk along the beach and soak up the warm Florida sunshine. It was January when he finally boarded a lumber schooner for Cuba.

Cuba offered John beaches, hills, and forests to roam. But malarial attacks continued to cause him feverish nightmares.

51

"Wrong climate, son," the ship's captain said. "If I was you, I'd head for snow country. You like mountains and woods and you'll find plenty of both out West."

By the middle of February, 1868, John Muir was on a steamer headed for New York. During a heavy storm off Cape Hatteras, John clung to the mast and let the cold wind and rain cool his fevered brow.

In New York, the ship's captain let John stay on board at night. During the day, he wandered around the cement "forest," which wouldn't be so bad, he thought, if it weren't for the people.

On March 10, he boarded the *Nebraska* for Aspinwall and from there by way of the Isthmus of Panama to San Francisco and the wilds of the West.

7

Climb the mountains
and get their good tidings.
Nature's peace will flow into you
as sunshine flows into trees.
The winds will blow
their own freshness into you,
and the storms their energy,
while cares drop off
like autumn leaves.

7

John was happy to set foot on the wharf at San Francisco. His steerage companions had been, as he wrote in one of his journals, ". . . a barbarous mob, especially at meal times."

"Well, 'ere we are," commented a Cockney named Chilwell. John had made friends with him aboard ship.

"And here we go," John replied, stopping a man on Market Street. "Excuse me, but which is the quickest way out of town?"

"Depends, I suppose, on where you're headed."

"Anyplace that is wild," John answered.

"Yes, well"—the stranger glanced nervously around —"why don't you go to the end of Market Street and take the Oakland Ferry?"

John and Chilwell landed on the Oakland side of the Bay and began tramping toward oak-covered hills to the south. The air was alive with larks singing what John considered their welcome song.

The men then walked eastward from Gilroy and climbed Pacheco Pass. It was spring of 1868 and John looked at what appeared to be blankets of wild flowers. "Look at that, Chilwell, a lake of pure golden sunshine."

"You sure got a fancy way of talkin'." Chilwell seemed amused. He waved his arm in an arc. "That's California's Great Central Valley."

"And that?" John pointed east to a mountain range in the distance.

"That'd be the Sierras. Some folks call it the Snowy Range, some the Sierra Nevadas."

John stared for a long time into the distance. "Just look at that!" He pointed toward the base of the range. "See how the colors blend? There at the bottom, a deep purple-rose. And there where the trees are thickest, a darker purple. And on up toward the sky the color changes to a soft blue, up to the pearl-gray snow."

"It's just a mountain, Muir." Chilwell shook his head and grinned.

"Nope." John continued to stare. "It's more than that — it's a Range of Light. That's where I'm going."

John and Chilwell descended from Pacheco Pass, across the Merced River into Yosemite Valley. Wherever they walked, John thought it seemed like walking in liquid gold. The air was alive with fragrance, singing larks, and wild bees. Rabbits and small bands of antelope blended into nature's symphony.

John searched where they had just seen a band of antelope. "What don't you see?" he asked Chilwell.

"Huh?"

John laughed. "I mean, look"—he pointed to the ground—"you don't see a crushed flower or weed."

"So?" Chilwell asked.

"There is no sign of destruction by the antelope, yet look at our tracks. Nature takes care of its own. Only man destroys."

Nature helped cool John's malarial fever with mountain winds and clear, crystal waters. Only ten days in Yosemite Valley and he felt like a new man.

"What now?" Chilwell asked. "I'm getting tired of all

56

this quiet and communin' with nature."

"I want to go on into the mountains, but first I'll need some supplies. Let's go back to Snelling . . . "

"We could get work harvesting," Chilwell said. "When I get paid, I'm going back to San Francisco—city wildness is more to my likin'."

When harvesttime ended, John and Chilwell parted company. "Sure don't know what's so all-fired interesting back there." Chilwell jerked a thumb over his shoulder toward the mountains.

"Nature, Chilwell—nature as God created it. The influences of pure nature stimulate the mind. This, my friend, is truly God's country." John shook hands with his friend.

John continued to work at sheepshearing and gentling wild horses. Then he went to the ranch of Pat Delaney, near La Grange. Still his thoughts were of the Sierras. Late in the fall he hired out to Smoky Jack Conncl as a sheepherder.

"Got about eighteen hundred sheep needs tending. There's a cabin you can live in"—Smoky Jack lighted his pipe, then pointed toward Snelling—"about two miles out that way."

John agreed, hoping to be closer to the wilderness. His first disappointment came as he approached the cabin. Scattered over the ground were old shoes, trash, ashes, sheep skeletons, and rams' horns. His second disappointment was the cabin itself. John best described it in his journal: "Generations of shepherds had left the cabin in a state of inconceivable filth."

John lived in loneliness for five months. But he found beauty and contentment a short distance from the cabin. He observed translucent silver mists settling over the rocks and hills. He listened to the music of the wind accented by deep thunder growls and crashes overhead as torrential rains pushed toward spring.

He watched delicate ferns unroll, adding lace to rocks. Boulders in creek beds came alive with purple mushrooms, liverworts, and mosses. Newborn insects tried their freshly dried wings in rhythm to the meadowlarks' liquid melodies. Life had returned to nature's children, the birds, flowers, and insects. "Lambs," John wrote, "salvaged from death feel skippy and gay, and they run in bands around the clay bank, dancing as if they were daft!"

8

This grand show is eternal.
It is always sunrise somewhere;
the dew is never dried at once;
a shower is forever falling;
vapor is ever rising.
Eternal sunrise, eternal sunset,
eternal dawn and gloaming,
on sea and continents and islands,
each in its turn,
as the round earth rolls.

David (Skipp) Weaver

**Summer in the Sierras
seemed like paradise
to Muir**

8

It was on June 3, 1869, that John began his first summer in the Sierras. He was once again working for Pat Delaney. They set out on the sheep caravan with blankets, camp kettles, and John's plant press. The sheep headed toward the tawny foothills. Following their puffs of dust rode Pat Delaney, looking, as John noted in his journal, "bony and tall, with sharply hacked profile like Don Quixote." Next came Billy, a shepherd who would do the work under John's supervision, then a digger Indian and a Chinese who would help the driving for a few days toward Tuolumne Meadows. Finally came John, his journal tied to his belt.

It was near nightfall when Mr. Delaney pointed to a hopper-shaped hollow at the foot of Pilot Peak Ridge. "We'll make camp there," he said.

The band of sheep nibbled grasses along the North Fork of the Merced River, while Billy set up racks for provisions in the shade of riverbank trees.

John feasted his eyes, heart, lungs, and mind with beauty and pure mountain air. At last he had reached paradise. He began gathering cedar plumes and fern fronds for a bed. Sleep came, deep and peaceful, under the trees and stars after John had been lulled by the hushed harmony of waterfalls and the soft sounds of night.

The men woke to a calm, cloudless warm day. "This

is what I've waited for—wild serenity!" John said.

"Gets even wilder." Pat Delaney jerked his head back, indicating the mountains. "Don't guess anyone but Yosemite Indians ever been deep into them."

"I will be one day," John called over his shoulder as he strode toward the river. He sat on a huge boulder at the bend in the river and wrote in his journal: " . . . over the hills, in the ground, in the sky, spring work is going on with joyful enthusiasm, new life, new beauty, unfolding, unrolling in glorious exuberant extravagance—new birds in their nests, new winged creatures in the air, and new leaves, new flowers, spreading, shining, rejoicing—everywhere."

Although John found beauty in nature and described it in almost poetic terms, he had a great sense of humor. This side of John Muir's character is best shown by his own description of the shepherd Billy from his journal, *My First Summer in the Sierra:*

"Our shepherd is a queer character and hard to place in this wilderness. His bed is a hollow made in red dry-rot punky dust beside a log which forms a portion of the south wall of the corral. Here he lies with his wonderful everlasting clothing on, wrapped in a red blanket, breathing not only the dust of the decayed wood but also that of the corral, as if determined to take ammoniacal snuff all night after chewing tobacco all day. Following the sheep he carries a heavy six-shooter swung from his belt on one side and his luncheon on the other. The ancient cloth in which the meat, fresh from the frying-pan, is tied serves as a filter through which the clear fat and gravy juices drip down on his right hip and leg in clustering stalactites. This oleaginous formation is soon broken up, however, and diffused and rubbed evenly into

62

his scanty apparel, by sitting down, rolling over, crossing his legs while resting on logs, etc., making shirt and trousers watertight and shiny. His trousers, in particular, have become so adhesive with the mixed fat and resin that pine-needles, thin flakes and fibers of bark, hair, mica scales and minute grains of quartz, hornblende, etc., feathers, seed-wings, moth and butterfly wings, legs and antennae of innumerable insects, or even whole insects such as the small beetles, moths and mosquitoes, with flower petals, pollen dust and indeed bits of all plants, animals, and minerals of the region adhere to them and are safely imbedded, so that though far from being a naturalist he collects fragmentary specimens of everything and becomes richer than he knows. His specimens are kept passably fresh, too, by the purity of the air and the resiny bituminous beds into which they are pressed. Man is a microcosm, at least our shepherd is, or rather his trousers. These precious overalls are never taken off, and nobody knows how old they are, though one may guess by their thickness and concentric structure. Instead of wearing thin they wear thick, and in their stratification have no small geological significance."

John put his stubby pencil in his shirt pocket when Mr. Delaney came up to him. "There's great fishin' and huntin' around here, John. If you'd like, I'll leave my rifle and you can . . . ."

"Let the hunter go into the Lord's woods and kill the beasts or wild Indians—not me!"

Pat Delaney laughed. "That's good, but there's nothing wrong with a man hunting. Makes a man right proud to come home with a good kill."

John shook his head. "I have no sympathy for the

selfish pride of civilized man."

Pat Delaney scratched his head. "You're a strange man."

"Tell you something else. If a war broke out between the wild beasts and man, I'd be tempted to sympathize with the beasts."

"Ah, come on! God put animals on earth for man's use. I don't agree with useless killin', but . . . "

"But nothing!" John stood up and ambled to the river's edge. "It's the devil's work to slaughter for sport. Let man slaughter beasts and it's fine. But let a bear kill a man! That's horrible. Maybe man was created for animals, and thanks be to God for claws and long, sharp teeth."

"Well, what about sheep? They provide us with food and wool."

"And money," John said. "It's not only animals, Mr. Delaney. Hemp is used for ship's rigging, tying packages, and hanging criminals. Cotton for clothing, iron for plows, and, ironically, lead for bullets—all provided for us."

"So?" A note of irritation was clear in Mr. Delaney's voice.

"But what of the creatures that do not fit into the category of man's needs? Lions, bears, tigers which smack their lips over raw man—insects that destroy man's crops and drink man's blood—wouldn't you say man was provided for *their* food and drink?"

"That's ridiculous!"

"I don't think so. Why does water"—John pointed to the river—"drown man? Why are some minerals poison to him?"

David (Skipp) Weaver

One of the "sparkling lakes"
that inspired Muir—
South Lake in the Sierras
with Bishop Pass in the background

Exploring wilderness areas like this one
along the Peshtigo River
deepened young John Muir's love of nature
as he grew up on a Wisconsin farm

Leaving his job, Muir wandered
south from Wisconsin to Florida,
through the "wildest, leafiest
world he had ever seen"

David (Skipp) Weaver

An eye injury filled young Muir
with fear that he would never again see
the "sweet . . . sights of nature,"
but he was cured to enjoy
Sierra trails like this

David (Skipp) Weaver

One of the majestic Sierra sights
that thrilled Muir was Fin Dome
near Rae Lakes

David (Skipp) Weaver

To the naturalist, running water was
both a theme in the orchestrated music
of nature and one of her instruments
for "carving the lines of mountains"

The winds of the Grand Canyon called
strongly too and finally the Muirs
moved to Arizona where the dry desert
air was better for Helen's health

David (Skipp) Weaver

After his wife's death, Muir returned
to the High Sierras and though
the great trees taught him
that life had to go on,
they could not console him

"I wouldn't know—I'm just a simple sheepman, not a philosopher."

"Well, I grant you, Mr. Delaney, the universe would be incomplete without man—but it would also be incomplete without the smallest creature."

"You're not strange, Muir." Delaney looked for a few minutes at John. "You're either a saint, a devil, or just plain crazy."

Delaney, the Chinese and the Indian returned to the ranch, leaving John with Billy. He tried to interest Billy in nature.

"How'd you like to go into Yosemite with me?"

Billy grinned. "What's there but a lot of rocks, a hole in the ground, and a darned good place to fall and break your fool neck. I say keep out."

John was alone in his adventurous thoughts. One afternoon he wandered away from camp and watched a bear from behind a tree. An idea came to John—he would make the bear run. He rushed from behind the tree and froze. The bear calmly stood up on his hind legs and stared at John. After several minutes of staring, the bear eased himself to all four feet and ambled leisurely off into the woods. John had won—each creature respected the other.

John experienced many nature trips during his first summer in the Sierras. Every hour of every day brought him new wonders. To him, every sight, sound, and smell in the Sierras was full of divine lessons.

One afternoon John climbed on top of a square-cut boulder in the Merced River. He later described it as being " . . . soothingly, restfully cool beneath the leafy, translucent ceiling." To John the water was delightful

65

music: " . . . the deep bass tones of the fall, the clashing ringing spray, and infinite variety of small low tones of the current gliding past the side of the boulder island. . . . The place seemed holy, where one might hope to see God."

Later that night, after Billy had gone to sleep, John went back to his boulder-island and spent the night with stars peering through the leafy roof.

The glorious days of summer faded into fall. The call of the winds seemed to cry out to John to stay and see the birds, animals, and forests in their snow-laden winter wonderland.

"Time to get these sheep back to the lowlands, John." Billy appeared overjoyed at the idea of leaving the high meadows. "Civilization again. Say good-by to your precious wilderness."

John's voice saddened. "If I had a few sacks of flour, an ax, and some matches, I'd stay right here."

"You're crazy."

"You're right!" John turned his head toward the Yosemite where he had seen the wonders of El Capitan and Half Dome, gazed up more than six hundred feet at Bridal Veil Falls and at Yosemite Falls. "I haven't seen any of the big trees yet. I'd head over the ridge to Wawona to the sequoias."

"And get lost and freeze to death. There's nothing up there."

"I'll come back, Billy. No place on earth is so overwhelmingly attractive as that hospitable Godful wilderness. Tracks and trails up there are nature's ornamental stitchery. But down there"—John looked toward the lowlands—"man blasts roads out of solid rock, builds dams to tame streams, . . . works mines like slaves. Man strips the face of the earth for his own convenience."

Billy shrugged and began rounding up the sheep. As a gentle breeze blew past John, he whispered to it, "I'll be back."

9

In God's wilderness lies the hope
of the world—the great fresh,
unblighted, unredeemed wilderness.
The galling harness
of civilization drops off,
and the wounds heal
ere we are aware.

David (Skipp) Weaver

The call of the winds kept Muir
in the wilderness of the Sierras
nine years, collecting specimens
and studying rock formations
on mountains like Whitney

9

John kept the promise he whispered to the wind. The call of the wild kept him in the mountains for nine years. He began his famous John Muir Trail at Glacier Point, then traveled north to Tuolumne Meadows, then turned south down to Whitney Portal.

John walked for weeks on end, collecting all the data and specimens he felt were necessary to teach people the values of the wilderness. He did not take the supplies that backpackers take along today. He took only a few toilet articles, a change of socks and underwear. A rolled blanket was all he needed for his bed. His food was simply tea and dried bread. "Dried bread keeps without getting moldy," he once explained. He carried a small kettle, a knife which he used only for whittling kindling, matches, and an ice ax. Of course, he was never without his journal, plant press, and magnifying glass.

"How come only one blanket?" he was often asked.

"My campfire keeps me warm. Pitch pine makes a nice hot fire even in rainy weather. When the rain pours or the snow falls, I find a cave or a fallen log big enough to make a roof."

A place to sleep never worried John. His days were filled with learning what Mother Nature had to teach. He played his magnifying glass over shiny granite rocks and wondered about the strange stripes in parallel lines. Then his attention turned to other rocks and boulders

71

of entirely different substance. "These must have been broken off cliffs in another part of Yosemite," he spoke to a Douglas squirrel that scampered by. "But how did they get here?"

Only one way, he decided after careful study. A forceful river of glacial ice must have swept down from the mountains thousands of years before. Only such an act of nature could have carved Yosemite Valley. John had read *The Yosemite Guide-Book*, written by Professor Josiah D. Whitney, state geologist of California. Whitney claimed that the bottom of the valley had simply sunk to an unknown depth as a result of a gigantic earthquake.

John refused such theory and turned to writing articles based on his own observations. "When we walk the pathways of Yosemite glaciers and contemplate their separate works—the mountains they have shaped, the canyons they have furrowed . . . instead of being overwhelmed as at first with its uncompared magnitude, we ask, *Is this all?* wondering that so mighty a concentration of energy did not find yet grander expression."

Although not a geologist, John recognized that such grandeur could not have been formed by cataclysmic earthquakes. Modern geologists agree that John Muir came much closer to the truth than did Professor Whitney. Modern methods have proven that both Whitney and Muir were correct. Glacier action was the main force in forming Yosemite Valley, but nature had assistance from cataclysmic causes. These John would have justified as also being an act of nature.

John's main interest concerned the spiritual beauty of nature, and his many journals, articles, sketches, and books have more than proven that.

72

He wrote the following primitive poem in his journal, perhaps because he felt that poetry best expressed his feelings for nature:

> The Valley is tranquil and sunful
> And Winter delayeth his coming.
> The river sleeps currentless in deep mirror pools,
> The falls scarce whisper.
> The brown meadows bask,
> The domes bathe dreamily in deep azure sky,
> And all the day is Light.

Critics often find fault with the writing of John Muir, but none can question his ability to describe nature in a beautiful way. John himself realized that his dependence on such adjectives as "glorious" and "beautiful" was a fault.

The development of John's writing was greatly aided by the arrival in Yosemite of Ralph Waldo Emerson. The two men became great friends. John acknowledged Emerson as a "master." It was after his meeting with Emerson that John entered in his journal the following thoughts concerning science and man: "The astronomer looks high, the geologist low. Who looks between on the surface of the earth? The farmer, I suppose, but too often he sees only grain, and of that only the mere bread-bushel-and-price side of it."

10

This star, our own good earth,
made many a successful journey
around the heavens ere man was made,
and whole kingdoms of creatures
enjoyed existence and returned
to dust ere man appeared
to claim them. After human beings
have also played their part
in Creation's plan, they too
may disappear without any
general burning or extraordinary
commotion whatever.

10

≈≈≈≈≈≈≈≈≈≈≈≈≈≈

Not one merely to write about the wilderness, John had to experience every facet of nature. His first earthquake happened while he slept. He opened his eyes and sat up. Low rumbling and wild rolling movement filled him with a strange combination of joy and fear. "A noble earthquake!" he later wrote in his journal. But at the moment, the earthshocks were violent and varied and came so close together that walking was difficult.

Outside his cabin, near Sentinel Rock, John noticed a calm, silent moonlit atmosphere. The earth stopped its movement, then another muffled rumbling ran underground and from the silence came a thundering roar. Eagle Rock, a short distance up the valley, surrendered to the earthquake and as John braced himself against a tree he watched huge boulders spill, bounce, and jump to the valley floor. In later describing the scene, John said, "Thousands of great boulders I had studied so long, poured to the valley floor in a free curve luminous from friction, making a terribly sublime and beautiful spectacle—an arc of fire fifteen hundred feet span, as true in form and as steady as a rainbow, in the midst of the stupendous roaring rockstorm."

John hurried down the trail, pausing at each aftershock and listening to the pines and oaks rustle their branches. He continued down the trail toward the small settlement centered around James Hutchings' sawmill where he worked from time to time.

"Guess you'll believe Whitney now," Hutchings called to John as he approached the group standing around the small hotel.

John walked calmly up to Hutchings and looked at the frightened faces around him. "No sign of the bottom dropping out up there," he said.

"Cathedral Dome could come crashing down and bury us all." Hutchings' voice trembled in his obvious terror.

John began to laugh. "Then I'd suggest you all get through the pass as quickly as you can."

"It's not funny," someone yelled. "Mr. Whitney said that's how—"

"Whitney!" John said, anger creeping into his voice. "Whitney's earthquake theory is no more the truth than the Indian's legends about angry spirits. This is a wonderful spectacle . . ."

Before John could finish, a second series of tremors hit. Somewhere in the distance a tree crashed to the ground.

"It's nothing to fear," John said. "Old Mother Nature is only trouncing us on her knee."

Another example of Mother Nature's trouncing came to John in December. He wandered up a hillside just as the morning sun warmed the frost. The air was crisp and birds voiced their approval of a rare California winter day. As he walked along he was aware of a strong wind stirring the leaves.

John rounded a crest, expecting more beauty, but horror made him sick. Below him, desolate earth lay

78

pockmarked where giant cavities had been dug into the mountain.

Trees, hacked and dynamited, lay like giant skeletons across ugly craters. "Man!" John shivered. "Centuries," he cried out to the wind, "it took centuries for trees to grow that big and in man's greed for gold it took only hours to destroy it."

"Pill-ooo-eeet!" screamed a Douglas squirrel, its teeth bared, fur bristling, dark eyes blazing.

"I'm glad you agree, my friend," John said and turned away from the scene. The wind grew in strength and stung against his cheeks. His long hair flew like streamers behind him.

John dashed into the heart of the woods amid falling, scattering oak leaves and pinecones. Pine needles flashed around him. Pollen, moss, and flecks of bracken filled the air. Trees crashed to the ground. John had to force his weight against the wind to keep on his feet. Sugar pines bowed gracefully almost to the ground. Douglas spruces waved their arms. Silver pines rippled like goldenrods.

"Nature is having a festival," John called out, "and even the most rigid giant tingles with excitement."

He wanted to learn all he could about the show that nature was building. The wind whipped his hair and tore at his clothes. He glanced around to find a tall Douglas spruce and began climbing. Hoisting himself from branch to branch, he reached the topmost, over a hundred feet up.

John braced himself like a squirrel. The movement was fantastic. He gyrated, flapped, bent, and swirled in ever-changing patterns as though he were attached to the tree like one of its branches.

As he looked out over the lower ridges, the rippling forests reminded him of a field of waving wheat. Sunlight, reflected from tossing pine branches, shone so brilliant that the earth seemed shrouded in snow. He marveled at the rainbow of color, purple-brown tree trunks, chocolate-colored manzanitas, yellows and crimsons blended with laurel grays.

John closed his eyes and listened to the wild woodwinds in symphony. The metallic click of pine needles softened by the rustle of laurels, the fluted whistle of pine boughs accented by bass booms of oak limbs—all blending.

All too soon, John thought, the symphony ended, not abruptly, but gently sighing into a thin breeze.

11

No synonym for God is so perfect
as Beauty. Whether as seen
carving the lines of the mountains
with glaciers, or gathering
matter into stars, or planning
the movements of water,
or gardening—still all is Beauty!

11

John left the Sierras in May of 1879 and boarded a steamer, *Dakota*, for Alaska. He made a stop in Oregon to observe the grandeur of its mountains and forests. He arrived in Alaska at Fort Wrangell in July. There he met Reverend Samuel Hall Young, a Presbyterian missionary, who was to share many of John's Alaskan adventures.

In mid-October, John and Sam set out with native paddlers to the north. As the small party approached Glacier Bay the Indian paddlers expressed deep-noted fear.

"Devilfish wait. Devilfish kill!"

"What are they talking about?" John asked Sam.

"These Indians are superstitious," Sam explained. "They believe a devilfish with arms as long as a tree lurks in these waters waiting to swallow up any unwary canoe."

John recorded the following in his journal, when the party had made camp: "After supper, crouching about a full fire of fossil wood, they [the Indians] became still more doleful, and talked in tones that accorded well with the wind and waters and growling torrents about us, telling sad old stories of crushed canoes, drowned Indians, and hunters frozen in snowstorms."

"Time to turn in," John finally called out.

"We not sleep," the Indians chorused.

"Now what?" John looked at Sam.

"Maybe they think a mischievous fairy, half man and half otter, will carry them away if they sleep."

"No wonder they beg for missionaries and teachers," John smiled slightly. "Still it seems they need more. Their superstitions are harmless."

"But unchristian," Sam said.

"Too often Christianizing savages makes them very nearly nothing. They lose their wild instincts and gain a hymnbook . . . they mope and doze and die on the outskirts of civilization like tamed eagles in barnyard corners, with blunt talons, blunt bills, and clipped wings."

"Perhaps you have a point." It was Sam's turn to smile slightly. "But without missionaries and teachers the Indians would have no protection from whiskey-soaked traders—and they, my friend, present a far greater and real evil than superstition."

Early one Sunday morning while the camp rested, John stretched his long legs and began to climb a fifteen-hundred foot ridge. He pushed through rain, mud, and snow, up the mountain slope. He jumped boulder-choked torrents, waded and wallowed in snow up to his shoulders. When he reached the peak he felt disappointment at the cloud-smothered landscape. But before long the clouds drifted higher and John saw an awe-inspiring sight. Below was an iceberg-filled expanse of bay and five huge glaciers. This was his first view of Glacier Bay, and he was the first white explorer to see the great solitude of ice. On February 25, 1925, forty-six years later, Glacier Bay became a national monument.

Later on this same journey, John discovered a great ice river that became known as Muir Glacier. He would have a lot to write about, so he decided to visit his friends, the Carrs, in Oakland, California.

John sailed back to San Francisco and ferried across the Bay to Oakland. After a few days in a rented room, trying to write, he called on Mrs. Carr. He had kept up correspondence with his family and the Carr family throughout his travels.

John never considered himself a writer. "Every time I try to describe nature, adjectives seem to crawl all over me. Mr. Emerson said I use too many."

"Relax, John. Forget your writing for a while." Mrs. Carr led him into the parlor.

"I can't. The editor of *Overland* wants my 'Studies in the Sierra' right away." He sat on the sofa and noticed a strange smile on Mrs. Carr's face. People only sat in parlors on formal occasions.

"I'm sure a day or two will not make any difference." Mrs. Carr stood looking out of the window. "Oh, good, here they come."

John jumped up. "I didn't know you were expecting company. I'll come back—"

"Now just sit right back down and relax." She went into the hall to welcome her guests.

John ran nervous fingers through his hair. He hated formality and felt trapped.

"John"—Mrs. Carr ushered three people into the parlor—"I'd like you to meet Dr. and Mrs. Strentzel."

"I've heard of your scientific work with orchards," John said, shaking hands with Dr. Strentzel.

"Most of the credit is due my daughter Louie." Dr. Strentzel stepped aside as Louie Wanda Strentzel stepped forward.

John smiled at the dark-haired, gray-eyed young lady.

85

Beautiful, ran through his mind, but all that came out of his mouth was, "Hello."

The afternoon passed too quickly for John. When the company left, Mrs. Carr asked, "Well, John, what do you think?"

"They are lovely people." John felt his face getting warm with embarrassment.

"And Louie?"

"Dr. Strentzel is right, you know. Conservation must be practiced in orchards and the woods. I think his—"

"And Louie?"

John wished Mrs. Carr would not be so persistent. "I'm going back to my room now and write so I can get back to the winds in the woods." He started for the door and turned back. "And Louie is beautiful," he said and left.

John found writing his articles easier. Maybe, he thought, it was what Louie had told him: "You have something of great importance to say, Mr. Muir—and the best way is just to say it."

John then returned to Alaska and joined Reverend Young on more explorations. John's enthusiasm was as keen as ever, but there was a memory even the wonders of Alaska could not erase. A beautiful face.

On April 14, 1880, John and Louie were married. Nature, as John loved it, seemed to approve. Rain poured down. The river overflowed, but to John it was a beautiful day.

John and Louie settled on a ranch in Martinez to raise fruit. A mutual understanding between husband and wife allowed John freedom to travel. While the grapes were ripening from July to October he was free to pursue his wilderness wandering.

86

There was still a lot of Alaska wilderness he wanted to see and explore. "I'm not through wandering," he said to Louie one evening as they sat on the ranch porch.

"I know"—Louie looked out over the cherry trees—"your heart is out there in the mountains."

"I'm sorry." John was proud of his work on the ranch and he was happy with Louie. Like his beloved trees he too had roots.

"John Muir, don't you ever be sorry for being what you are. I would be terribly unhappy if ever you felt your roots were shackles." Louie laughed, and placed her hand on his. "You're so like the wind—wild and free."

"Well, I'd like to go back to Alaska."

"Then go. Just be careful."

12

The mountains are fountains
of men as well as of rivers,
of glaciers, of fertile soil.
The great poets, philosophers,
prophets, able men whose thoughts
and deeds have moved the world,
have come down from the mountains—
mountain-dwellers who have
grown strong there with the forest
trees in Nature's work-shops.

12

Miles of glaciers thousands of feet thick welcomed John as they ground down from icy summits to the ocean. With Reverend Young, he set out in canoes to Sum Dum Day. John, never interested in what he called "the mere bread-bushel-and-price side of nature," recognized the possibility of gold in the gravelly creek beds. He mentioned his observations to a couple of prospectors, who proved John to be right. The historic stampede for gold that followed led to the founding of Juneau, Alaska.

John's second trip to Alaska was highlighted by a small shaggy black dog named Stickeen. Stickeen belonged to another member of the expedition, but soon adopted John, following him everywhere.

One morning John set out from Taylor Bay to explore a huge glacier. "Go back, Stickeen," John scolded in his sternest voice, but he had to hide a laugh as Stickeen sat and stared up at him, then suddenly bounced ahead. Stickeen turned and barked once, then raced toward the glacier.

"For a two-year-old you're sure stubborn." John's laugh was all Stickeen needed to know that he had won.

John carefully circled twenty- and thirty-foot-wide crevasses that went down a thousand feet or more, but easily jumped across those two to eight feet wide. Stickeen ran, stretched out his short legs, and made each leap right beside John. It took the pair three hours to cover seven miles of ice and snow. John explored branches of the glacier while his canine friend sniffed and snorted as though he too were exploring.

"Let's get back to camp, Stickeen," John called and began his descent by a different route. The crevasses were wider, and a few times John narrowly escaped plunging to his death. Stickeen showed no sign of fear as he kept pace. Then they came upon a crevasse too long to go around and too wide to jump. "There's an ice bridge," John spoke gently to Stickeen, who stuck his nose over the edge and whimpered. There was an eight-foot drop from surface to bridge. "Kinda droops in the middle—I'd say about thirty feet." He scratched Stickeen's neck, gave it a firm pat and set to work.

John cut a deep hollow on the brink for his knees, then leaned over and with his ice ax cut a step about seventeen inches down. Next he moved cautiously down and repeated cutting steps until he reached the bridge. The abyss on either side seemed bottomless. John ignored everything but the slippery bridge. He balanced himself by pressing his knees firmly on each side and inched his way across, then chipped steps up to the top.

John heard Stickeen's frightened howls from across the crevasse. "Come on, boy," John called. "You can make it." But the dog lay at the edge and howled even louder.

"Stickeen!" John's voice, firm but calm, tried to encourage the dog. "It's easy, boy. Nothing to be afraid of."

Stickeen stood, poised himself at the edge, then pushed himself back as fast as his short legs could manage. His howls grew louder, more pleading.

"All right, stay there," John finally called and walked out of Stickeen's sight, hoping the frightened animal would find courage from facing abandonment. On the wind came almost human wailing and moaning. Once again John called, this time more commanding. "Your last chance, Stickeen. I'll come back in the morning, and, if you're not frozen, I'll . . ." John held his breath. Stickeen began slowly inching to the edge. "That's it," John continued to talk, while the dog cautiously slipped over the edge and picked his way by the steps to the bridge. Stickeen paused, glanced up at John through the snow that had begun to fall, then paced himself step by step across the icy bridge. Once again fawn-colored eyes glanced up. "Almost here." John leaned as far over to the edge as he could and patted one of the steps. "Come on." After a few moments of silent pleading, Stickeen glanced back at the bridge he had just crossed, then up at the steps and notches as though counting them. With amazing speed he scrambled up and over the edge.

Stickeen shot past John and began to run in giddy circles, shoveling his nose into the snow, then rolling over and over, yelping, screaming, and barking. Finally, he ran several yards ahead of John, turned sharply, ran toward him and leaped up into John's arms with such force that man and dog rolled in the snow, laughing, yelping, screaming, and shouting.

Years later John wrote a small book entitled *Stickeen*, published in 1909. It had taken him twenty-nine years to write it.

All in all, John made five trips to Alaska, which resulted in many articles and the books *The Cruise of the*

Corwin and *Travels in Alaska*. His adventures on the Harriman expedition of 1899 he put into *John of the Mountains*.

In March of 1881 John became the father of Annie Wanda Muir. His pride and happiness in fatherhood helped him remain at the Martinez farm to write his Alaska and Yosemite books.

Two important bills on conservation for Yosemite were before Congress. John had been trying for ten years to have these measures introduced.

"Don't know which is more important," he said to his wife.

"I should think the bill to enlarge Yosemite and the Mariposa Big Tree Groves," she smiled and poured him a cup of coffee.

"Yes, but enlarging the area doesn't help save natural resources. I think maybe the bill to create a California State Park should be first."

"Either one, John, I'm sure would make you happy." Louie sat across from him and began to sip her coffee. "Tell me about the Sierra Nevada."

"Well, take this piece of bread." John placed the slice in front of him and used his knife to illustrate. "If we cut the Sierra Nevada into blocks—say a dozen miles or so in thickness—each section would have a Yosemite Valley and a river together with lakes, meadows, and forests."

Louie nodded, her smile encouraging him to go on.

"Why, the grandeur of each block would be so vast and satisfying that to choose one spot would be like selecting slices of bread cut from the same loaf." He pointed his knife at the freshly baked loaf on the table.

"I'm sorry, dear, but I don't really see . . ."

94

"One slice," John hurried on, "might have burned spots, like craters, another might be more browned, another more raggedly cut or crusted—but don't you see, Louie, all would be essentially the same."

"I'm beginning to see."

"We'd all pick the Merced slice."

"Why?" Louie asked.

"Because access is easier, it's been nibbled and tasted and proven very good. And, because of the concentrated form of its Yosemite, caused by certain conditions of baking, yeasting, and glacier-frosting of this portion of the Sierra Nevada loaf."

"Beautiful, John, and I do see." Louie jumped up to take care of the needs of Annie Wanda.

"But people will eat the whole loaf," he called after Louie. "They're that greedy."

John had been right. Neither bill passed Congress, conservation of natural resources was of little importance to people.

John Muir and one of the majestic
sequoias that he treasured
and maneuvered to save
for future generations

13

Government protection should be
thrown around every wild grove
and forest on the mountains,
as it is around every private
orchard, and the trees in public parks.
To say nothing of their value
as fountains of timber, they are
worth infinitely more than all
the gardens and parks of towns.

13

In 1885, John Muir had to stop writing and working for conservation. His youngest sister Joanna had sent word that their father was seriously ill. John went back to Wisconsin.

"He's dying," Joanna told John and led him into their father's room.

"Is that my beloved John?" a weak voice asked.

"Yes, Father." John sat beside his father and took his hand.

"My dear wanderer," were the last words Daniel spoke to John.

After Daniel's death, John wept and he forgave his father for his lack of understanding and his cruel treatment.

John made a vow not only to understand his child but to help her understand nature. In 1886 his second daughter, Helen, was born and John kept his vow.

He taught his daughters the names of all the flowers around the ranch. "Nature is God's classroom," he told them.

It was for this vast classroom that John continued to fight. He had been asked to write articles for two nature-study volumes. It seemed to John he was fighting more than one losing battle.

"All this writing to do, and the ranch work—there's no time for freedom," he told Louie one evening.

"I know," she said, "and that's why we're going to sell off part of the ranch."

John shook his head. "This was your father's ranch and," he sighed, "it's a good money-maker."

"John Muir!" Louie almost shouted. "You dare express interest in making money?"

"Well, it's important to us . . ."

"No, it's not." Louie was firm. "What's important is your writing and your fight to save precious land. Tell the people how important conservation is. Our girls aren't going to starve, you know. You've worked hard all these years."

John's heart and mind were eased by Louie's bright smile. He knew from the twinkle in her gray eyes that she loved him and approved of his way of life.

With renewed effort John took up his fight. An associate editor of *Century Magazine*, Robert Johnson, invited him to San Francisco to discuss articles on conservation.

"Not here." John glanced around the room in the Palace Hotel in San Francisco. "I'd like to show you what I'll write about, Mr. Johnson. Come camping with me in Yosemite Valley."

"Great idea," Mr. Johnson readily agreed.

A few days later they sat beside a campfire. "John, you've shown me the sequoias and scenery that nearly defies description—but where are the lakes of flowering meadows you mentioned?"

John poked the fire. "Gone—beaten down by sheep and people." He pointed with a stick toward a field of hay. "Hotel people dynamited out trees to plant that for horses."

"But I understood the State took charge of all this

100

back in 1864." Mr. Johnson figured quickly in his head. "That's twenty-six years. If something isn't done, the sequoias will disappear as surely as . . ."

"The passenger pigeons." John ran his fingers through his hair. "Remember them?"

"So thick they nearly blotted out the sun," Mr. Johnson said. "Now they say there are only a few left." He stood and stretched, turned his back to the fire. "Only one thing to do—get this area declared a national park."

"How?" John asked. "Seems the government is content with its one national park, Yellowstone. Two bills were defeated before."

"This time Congress will pass them. It's up to us to see to it."

"Congress is too easily swayed by lobbyists. If only we could rally the people to—"

"We can," Johnson said. "We'll do some lobbying of our own. We'll start with your articles in *Century*, complete with illustrations."

The fight began in June of 1889, with the first victory on October 1, 1890, when the region surrounding Yosemite Valley became a national park. Congress passed laws making the General Grant and the Sequoia National Parks.

"You must be happy now," Louie said, "and mighty proud."

"I am, but so much more needs to be done. I've worked out a plan to nationalize Kaweah-Kings River area."

John's plan was defeated when this bill became buried in committees. John turned again to his friend Mr. Johnson.

"I'm sorry," he said, "this time the opposition was

101

ready for us. But we did do *some* good."

"Not enough, Mr. Johnson, we've got to fight on."

"We can't do it alone. What we need is organized help."

"Where can we get that kind of help?"

"The people. There are plenty of people who feel as you do about conservation. They'll help. Start an association to preserve our mountains and natural wonders."

"You mean a club?" John brightened. "Why not?"

In May of 1892, a small group assembled for the first meeting of the Sierra Club, with John as its first president. He held that office until he died.

"And just what is the purpose of your club?" his wife asked when he came home from that first meeting.

"To explore and enjoy the mountains—to get the people and the government to preserve forests and other natural beauties of the Sierras. Isn't it wonderful?" John grabbed his wife and danced all around the room.

"Well," Louie finally freed herself, "do you suppose that the president of the Sierra Club could possibly calm down long enough for dinner?"

14

These temple-destroyers,
devotees of ravaging commercialism,
seem to have a perfect contempt
for Nature, and, instead of
lifting their eyes to the God
of the mountains, lift them
to the Almighty Dollar.

The outdoorsman turned lobbyist and
politician to plead the case for making
national parks of wilderness areas
a full century before most people believed
open space could possibly be endangered

14

John and the Sierra Club won victories and suffered many defeats. In 1893, forest reserves of thirteen million acres had been set aside by the Federal Government. Still lumbermen and sheepmen trespassed.

John worked with a six-man commission appointed to survey other parts of the country. He discovered much of Wyoming's Big Horn Mountains to be a forest of stumps. The Black Hills of South Dakota were being ruined. Such conditions were found to exist in Montana, Idaho, Washington, and Oregon. The Grand Canyon in Arizona, although a federal reserve, had several mines operating in the canyon and its forests were being devastated.

"What good," John asked, "is a national forest or a federal reserve without protection?"

The commission report recommended military control with a Forest Bureau to be established as soon as possible. In February 1897 a preliminary copy of the Forestry Commission Report was sent to President Cleveland. It recommended:

1. The creation of thirteen new reservations distributed among eight Western States.
2. The repeal or modification of timber and mining laws leading to fraud and robbery.

105

3. The scientific management of forests to maintain a permanent timber supply.
4. The creation of two new national parks: Grand Canyon and Mount Rainier, with adjacent acres.

President Cleveland was so impressed that on February 22 he issued an Executive Order setting aside the thirteen reservations, a total of over twenty-one million acres.

Stock, mining, and lumber syndicates became so enraged that they bombarded senators and congressmen with pleas and threats to impeach President Cleveland.

The result was that the President's reserves were set aside by Congress, which voted to suspend the Executive Order until March 1, 1898. Then Cornelius Bliss, new Secretary of the Interior, withheld the Forestry Report from the public and opened the reserves to settlers.

John began a series of articles, "The American Forests," for *The Atlantic Monthly.* He included the Forestry Report in his articles. He went over the heads of Congress and struck home to the needs and rights of the common people.

"Every other civilized nation in the world," he wrote, "has been compelled to care for its forests. Our government, like a rich and foolish spendthrift, has allowed its heritage to be sold and plundered and wasted at will."

He ended this memorable article with an impassioned plea: "Any fool can destroy trees. They cannot run away; and if they could, they would still be destroyed—chased and hunted down as long as fun or a dollar could be got out of their bark hides, branching horns, or magnificent bole backbones. Through all the wonderful, eventful

106

centuries since Christ's time—and long before that—God has cared for these trees, but He cannot save them from fools—only Uncle Sam can do that."

Mount Rainier became a national park in 1899. The Grand Canyon was not made a national monument until 1908 and a national park in 1919. But John Muir had gained valuable ground in his fight.

He traveled all over the United States, working for conservation, fighting against syndicates and lobbyists, making friends with celebrities both in and out of government.

Through the people, his efforts changed the attitude of Congress. When Theodore Roosevelt became President, he persuaded Congress to create a Bureau of Forestry.

John's family had grown up, his daughters were proud of their father. Now the President of the United States had written to him.

"What does he want?" Helen leaned over the back of John's chair on the veranda.

"I'll know when I open it." John's finger trembled slightly as he ran it under the flap of the envelope. He was afraid the letter might mean more defeats or maybe create a delay in his plans for an around-the-world trip.

He had traveled to Europe in 1893 and visited his native Scotland, but there was more to see, and he had just passed his sixty-fifth birthday—time for travel was growing short.

John sighed deeply and pulled the letter from its envelope. He could hardly believe his eyes. "Read it, Helen." He handed the letter over his shoulder.

She mumbled through the words, her excitement climbing. Then she read slowly and clearly: "I do not

107

want anyone with me but you, and I want to drop politics for four days."

"Looks like I'm going to be President Roosevelt's personal guide." John walked to the veranda railing and leaned out to look at the mountains, moisture filling his eyes. His trip would have to wait—this was really important.

The President arrived and he and John stood chatting at the edge of the Mariposa Big Tree Grove. Two rangers, a cook, and the stage driver heaved baggage onto the stagecoach. Reporters and local politicians crowded around the coach that was to carry them all to Wawona.

"Mr. President," John whispered, "let's get a couple of horses from behind the stable. I want you to be free to see the Yosemite without all those reporters and . . ."

"Bully, Mr. Muir," Roosevelt grinned, "you're a man after my own heart."

The two rode off on that brisk May morning in 1903. John pointed out both beauty and devastation. That night John Muir and Theodore Roosevelt camped near Glacier Point in a meadow lined with fir trees.

"I'm afraid we forgot to bring tents," John said.

"Mr. Muir, who needs tents when we've got the stars. This is bully."

"It won't be bully for long," John said as the men prepared beds of fir needles and fern. "Every day more timber thieves, more destruction. Scenic spots are beaten down by saddle horses and pack mules. No public highways to keep people on a directed route. And the worst, Mr. President, are the fires left to go out of control because the Federal Government and the State aren't sure who owns the timber."

108

Later, President Roosevelt spoke of his adventure in the Yosemite with enthusiasm—enthusiasm for the wonders of nature and for their preservation. "I ask for the preservation of other forests on the grounds of wise and foresighted economic policy," he said in a speech in Sacramento and concluded in his typical booming, Roughrider voice, "We are not building this country of ours for a day. It is to last through the ages."

John read the President's speech in a newspaper. He lowered the paper to his lap and looked at Louie. "I think we've finally won."

15

All the merry dwellers of the trees
and streams, and the myriad swarms
of the air, called into life by
the sunbeam of a summer morning,
go home through death, wings folded
perhaps in the last red rays of sunset
of the day they were first tried.
Trees towering in the sky,
braving storms of centuries,
flowers turning faces to the light
for a single day or hour,
having enjoyed their share
of life's feast—all alike pass on
and away under the law of death
and love. Yet all are our brothers
and they enjoy life as we do,
share Heaven's blessings with us,
die and are buried in hallowed
ground, come with us out of
eternity and return into eternity.
"Our lives are rounded with a sleep."

15

John realized his desire to go around the world. He went again to Europe, then to Australia, India, Siberia, Egypt, Japan, and Hawaii. He compared the mountains and forests of the world. "Mighty as they are," he told his wife, "none have the majesty of the sequoias."

The fight to save the sequoias continued, with victory at last in 1905 when Yosemite Valley became controlled by the U.S. National Park Service.

Yet even in victory can come defeat. That same year Louie Muir became ill and died on August 6. John seemed lost for several months—even trips into the Sierras could not dim his heartache. But he knew life had to go on, just as it did in the forests.

John Muir's years after Louie's death were spent wandering in the Sierras, exploring Arizona, and writing. He moved his daughter Helen to a town near Daggett on the Mohave Desert because of her failing health— her lungs needed the dry air of the desert.

John then went to South America and to Africa. "It's as though the winds call me," he explained to Helen.

"I know," she said. "Sometimes I think you are the wind. And—I think it's calling you back to the Sierras."

Helen was right. John, satisfied that his daughter's health was greatly improved, returned to the mountains he loved so much. This time to Hetch Hetchy Valley,

113

a place that surpassed even Yosemite.

Hetch Hetchy Valley was the site chosen to be turned into a water reservoir for the city of San Francisco. President Roosevelt encouraged John to fight against the project—a fight that ended in John's greatest defeat. He had convinced President Taft that the valley should not be turned into a lake. But President Wilson in 1913 appointed Franklin Lane as Secretary of the Interior. Lane was a native of San Francisco and formerly its city attorney. Congress authorized the Hetch Hetchy reservoir.

"Dam Hetch Hetchy? As well dam for watertanks the people's cathedrals and churches, for no holier temple has ever been consecrated by the heart of man." These were John's final words on the subject.

John had grown tired; his life devoted to winds in the woods had reached its seventy-sixth year. He stayed on the Martinez ranch, working on his book *Travels in Alaska*. In December he decided to visit his daughter Helen and see his grandchildren.

Life had been good to him—he had won safety for many of nature's wonders. For his work he received honorary degrees from Harvard, Yale, the Universities of Wisconsin and California. Yet, greatest of all to him was the creation in 1908 of Muir Woods National Monument.

John's thoughts were of Christmas with Helen as the train rattled into Daggett. He stepped into a heavy rain and by the time he reached Helen's home he was drenched.

He caught a cold and developed pneumonia. Helen rushed him to a hospital in Los Angeles. For a few days it appeared that he would recover.

"We'll come back Christmas Day," Wanda and Helen promised.

John beamed at them. "I've got to work—make corrections on these typed pages of *Travels in Alaska*." Then his smile faded. "Wanda . . . Helen . . ." He looked at his daughters for a few seconds, then his smile returned. "Merry Christmas."

It was Christmas Eve. John glanced at the papers scattered over his hospital bed. He reached for a blank sheet of paper and wrote:

"Death is a kind nurse saying, 'Come, children, to bed, and get up in the morning'—a gracious Mother calling her children home."

John Muir leaned back on his pillow and went to sleep, a deep sleep from which he never awakened.

Chronology

1838	April 21, born in Dunbar, Scotland, to Daniel Muir and Ann Gilrye Muir.
1849	February 19, sailed from Glasgow, Scotland, to New York, then traveled to Buffalo Township, near Portage, Wisconsin, with his brother David, his sister Sarah, and his father.
1860	In September, exhibited his inventions at the Wisconsin State Agricultural Fair in Madison.
1861	In January, entered the University of Wisconsin.
1863	In June, left the University of Wisconsin with the idea of entering medical school at the University of Michigan.
1864–67	Botanized in Canada and worked at odd jobs; inventor in a broom factory, was offered a partnership in a carriage company in Indianapolis; temporarily lost his eyesight in an industrial accident; made his decision to devote his life to God's wilderness.
1867	From September 2, 1867, to January, 1868, made his famous thousand-mile walk from Indianapolis to Florida and from there sailed to Cuba.
1868	March 28, arrived in San Francisco, California. Went to work on a lowland sheep ranch.
1869	His first summer in the Sierras herding sheep.
1870	With LeConte geological expedition in the Yosemite.
1871	Emerson visited John Muir in Yosemite.
1871–75	Developed his glacial theory as the origin of Yosemite; a controversy with Josiah D. Whitney.
1874–76	Climbed Mount Shasta. Began serious study of trees. Began a movement for federal control of forests.
1877–78	His exploration of the Great Basin.

117

1879	His first Alaska trip, with S. Hall Young.
1880	April 14, married Louie Wanda Strentzel. In July, made second trip to Alaska; returned in September.
1881	Third trip to Alaska, aboard the *Corwin;* cruised the Arctic waters.
1882–87	Remained home and raised fruit.
1888	Climbed Mount Rainier.
1889	Worked toward creating Yosemite National Park.
1890	Congress passed the Yosemite National Park Bill. Muir explored Muir Glacier in Alaska.
1891–92	Founded the Sierra Club and worked for recession of Yosemite Valley.
1893–94	Made a visit to Europe. *The Mountains of California* first published.
1896–98	Received M.A. degree from Harvard and LL.D. degree from the University of Wisconsin. Worked with National Forest Commission.
1899	Member of the Harriman-Alaska Expedition.
1901–02	*Our National Parks* published. Began fight to save the Hetch Hetchy Valley.
1903–04	After guiding President Roosevelt through the Yosemite, made a world tour.
1905	August 6, Louie Strentzel Muir died. Yosemite Valley came under control of the U.S. National Park Service.
1906	Explored Arizona.
1909	*Stickeen* was published.
1911	*My First Summer in the Sierra* was published. Received Litt. D. degree from Yale.
1912	*The Yosemite* was published.
1913	*The Story of My Boyhood and Youth* was published. Lost fight to save Hetch Hetchy Valley. Received LL.D. degree from University of California.
1914	Died in Los Angeles, California, on Christmas Eve.

John Muir
Remembered on the Map

Mount Muir—Alaska

Mount Muir—California

Muir—a Santa Fe Railroad station

Muir Glacier—Alaska

Muir Glacier—Washington

Muir Gorge—California

Muir Grove—California

Muir Inlet—Alaska

John Muir High—California

John Muir Trail—High Sierra

Muir Lake—California

Muir Mountain—California

Muir Pass—California

Muir's Peak—California

Muir Point—Alaska

Muir Woods—California

Selected Bibliography

Atlantic Monthly, August, 1894.

Bade, William F., *The Life and Letters of John Muir,* Houghton Mifflin Company, 1923.

Colby, William E., "The Latest Evidence Bearing on the Creation of Yosemite Valley," *Yosemite Nature Notes,* Vol. XXXV, No. 1 (January, 1956).

Johnson, Robert Underwood, *Remembered Yesterdays.* Little, Brown & Company, 1925.

Muir, John, "John of the Mountains," *The Unpublished Journals of John Muir,* ed. by Linnie Marsh Wolfe. Houghton Mifflin Company, 1938.

——*The Mountains of California.* Century Company, 1894.

——*My First Summer in the Sierra.* Houghton Mifflin Company, 1911.

——*Stickeen: The Story of a Dog.* Houghton Mifflin Company, 1909.

——*The Story of My Boyhood and Youth.* Houghton Mifflin Company, 1913.

——*Travels in Alaska.* Houghton Mifflin Company, 1915.

Roosevelt, Theodore, *Autobiography.* Charles Scribner's Sons, 1906.

Teale, Edwin Way (ed.), *The Wilderness World of John Muir.* Houghton Mifflin Company, 1954.

Young, S. Hall, *Alaska Days with John Muir.* Fleming H. Revell Company, 1915.

Index

124

125